PARTINGTIME HALL

Partingtime Hall

POEMS BY
James Fenton
AND
John Fuller

Viking Salamander

First published in 1987 by
The Salamander Press, 18 Anley Road, London W14 0BY, England
in association with
Penguin Books Ltd, Harmondsworth, Middlesex, England
Viking Penguin Inc., 40 West 23rd Street, New York, New York
10010, U.S.A.
Penguin Books Australia Ltd, Ringwood, Victoria, Australia
Penguin Books Canada Limited, 2801 John Street, Markham, Ontario,
Canada L3R 1B4
Penguin Books (N.Z.) Ltd, 182–190 Wairau Road, Auckland 10,
New Zealand

ISBN 0 948681 05 5

Set in Linotron Sabon
by Rowland Phototypesetting (London) Ltd
Printed and bound in Britain
by Oxford University Press

'Poem against Catholics' first appeared in the *New Review*, 'Chlorine Gardens' in *Quarto*, and 'The Land of Leery Looks' in *Critical Quarterly*.

Contents

"The Cuttle-Fish, the Calamary, and the Polipus, have all three a Magazine of Ink, or Bladder full of a black Liquor, which proves of great service to them when in Danger of being caught."

Nature Display'd, 1736, iii. 180

The Thing that People Do

When God created Paradise,
As every child can tell,
He placed old Adam gardener
With a woman there as well.
Said God: "Enjoy yourself, me lad,
And enjoy your woman, too,
But never let me catch you at
The thing that people do."

Oh the thing that people do,
The thing that people do:
It's long-winded and it's difficult,
Like changing trains at Crewe,
So go enjoy yourself, me lad,
And enjoy your woman, too,
But never let me catch you at
The thing that people do!

"Lay off young Alcibiades,"
The Athenian court did say,
"And Socrates, just tell us why
Our lads turn out that way?
Euripedes? Eumenides!
It's an old, old tale but true.
We'll dose you up with hemlock for
The thing that people do."

Oh the thing some people do,
The thing some people do,
The thing you need the ointment for
If you don't want a botcheroo.
Euripedes? Eumenides!
It's an old, old tale but true
And we'll dose you up with hemlock for
The thing some people do.

Leander, growing weary, cried:
"This is quite beyond a joke.
It's saltier than the Hellespont.
I'll try just one more stroke,
But I'm in it up to the shoulder-blades
(I should have brought a canoe).
It'll come to a sticky end all right,
This thing that people do."

Oh the thing that people do,
The thing that people do!
It's deep and wet and dangerous,
With more than a whiff of glue.
But you're in it up to your shoulder-blades
And you wish you'd brought a canoe.
It'll come to a sticky end all right,
The thing that people do.

Once Mrs Patrick Campbell
Was alone with Bernard Shaw
She apologised profusely
As she dragged him to the floor:
"I'm Shavian under the armpits,
I'm Shavian through and through,
But what's the point without a bit of
The thing that Shavians do?"

Oh the thing that Shavians do,
The thing that Shavians do,
The thing they do with vegetables,
It tastes like Irish stew.
I'm Shavian under the armpits,
I'm Shavian through and through,
But what's the point without a bit of
The thing that Shavians do?

What Oscar Wilde and Bosie did
With their respective tools
Was certainly below the belt
And against the Queensberry rules.
"Oh Oscar Fingal O'Flaherty, dear,
Is it up to me, or to you?
Either way it's a bit outré,
The thing that aesthetes do."

Oh the thing that aesthetes do,
The thing that aesthetes do.
Some do it with great style. They use
A pubic hair shampoo.
But others simply steep the sheets
Now and then in Reckitt's Blue.
Whatever way, it's a bit outré,
The thing that aesthetes do.

And then there was Havelock Ellis
Who loved his consommé,
But whenever he tried to drink it
His beard got in the way.
Beards are more trouble than they're worth
When you're playing peekaboo
And hair gets simply everywhere in
The thing that people do.

Oh the thing that people do,
The thing that people do:
Such beastly consequences from
That fatal interview
When neither knows what the other wants
In the game of peekaboo
And everything gets everywhere in
The thing that people do.

When Lou Andreas-Salomé
Made her bid for Sigmund Freud,
She found his Pleasure Principle
Grotesquely unemployed.
Said Freud: "You did for Nietzsche
And you did for Rilke, Lou,
But mate, I've learned to sublimate
The thing that people do."

Oh the thing that people do,
The thing that people do.
Vienna is obsessed with it,
Like monkeys at the zoo.
It was good enough for Nietzsche.
It was great for Rilke, Lou,
But mate, I've learned to sublimate
The thing that people do.

When Lawrence of Arabia
Was roughed up by a turk
He made this bold confession
As the brute got down to work:
"I can do it with an earmuff,
I'm not bad with a shoe,
But tell me, how do people fit
In this thing that people do?"

Oh the thing that people do,
The thing that people do!
It's easy when you're on your tod,
Much trickier when there's two.
There's comfort in an earmuff.
There's triumph in a shoe.
But I just can't see how people fit
In this thing that people do.

Leda was always swanning about
And Irene gave in to Soames.
Ginger did it with William
And Watson did it with Holmes.
The Queen of England has done it
And someone does it with you:
But why on earth do they do it,
The thing that people do?

Oh the thing that people do,
The thing that people do.
Why did you have to remind us?
Why isn't the thing taboo?
Everyone does it to someone
And someone does it to you,
But why, why, WHY do they do it,
The thing that people do?

Chlorine Gardens, Belfast

Oh to live in Chlorine Gardens,
Where the brain leaps in the pan.
A hundred husbands' hundred hard-ons
Get it, as and when they can.
A myriad sins, a myriad pardons
Form the average Christian span.
Oh to live in Chlorine Gardens
Where a man can be a man!

Oh to live in Chlorine Gardens
Where a chap can read a book:
A bulging row of hard-back Ardens,
Both the Grigsons (how to cook
Spatch-cocked woodcock laced with lardons,
Fricassee of Lalla Rookh!)
Ah, the smells of Chlorine Gardens—
Lift the lid and take a look!

Lift the lid on Chlorine Gardens
Where the chess-buffs rise at dawn
To play old games of Leonard Barden's.
Their wives choose flip-sides with a yawn:
Their ears, and hearts, are Jack Teagarden's
While hubby touches up a pawn.
Oh what games in Chlorine Gardens!
No one ever mows the lawn.

No one mows those Chlorine Gardens
Where the sperm soars with the yeast.
Virginity like Dolly Varden's
Anticipates a midnight feast.
Each recondite position hardens
When the wind blows nor' nor' east.
Oh to sleep in Chlorine Gardens!
Few the sheets that stay uncreased.

Oh to sleep in Chlorine Gardens!
The minister is non-committal,
Murmuring, confidens et ardens:
"Wait while I slip into a little
Something of Teilhard de Chardin's."
God! On Sunday morning it'll
Be grand to live in Chlorine Gardens:
More theology, less spittle.

Yes. To live in Chlorine Gardens
Where the spirit comes on strongly
Not as in your Berchtesgadens
Where things somehow turned out wrongly.
Forget your Spas, your Baden-Badens
(All along, down-and-out along-lea):
Come and live in Chlorine Gardens
With Paul Muldoon and Edna Longley—

Yes, come and live in Chlorine Gardens
With Paul, and us, and Edna Longley.

From the Aztec

Aaeeyah! Time passes very slowly

tiquiti tiquiti
toquiti toquiti

I am lying on the sacrificial slab
and the High Priest Hotwoatlbotl stands over me
with his obsidian knife

tiquiti tiquiti
toquiti toquiti

he is wearing a blue robe
made from the pelts of a thousand kingfishers
and lined with the skins of a thousand axolotls!

tiquiti tiquiti
toquiti toquiti

I ask him where he got it

tiquiti tiquiti

he says the Princess Wotlotlgotl made it for him

toquiti toquiti
tiquiti tiquiti

I say:
If I gave her the kingfishers and the axolotls
would she make one for me
???

toquiti toquiti

He says:
Infidel!
One more word out of you
and I shall take my obsidian knife
and cut off your testicolotls!

tiquiti tiquiti
toquiti toquiti

Aaaeeeyah!

let me out of here

Nuns

The size of the Mother Superior
Made a tongue-job as weary, nay wearier
Than late Henry James,
The Commonwealth Games,
Or an evening of opera seria.

And at Vespers her singular shape
Was maintained with blind faith and scotch tape.
She kept up her form
Every night in the dorm
Till the novices shopped her for rape.

"Once again, dears, we're gathered for Nones.
Can't you feel the suspense in your bones?
Now take up your station
In mutual prostration.
Let the Chapel resound with your moans."

The organ was busy at Lauds
And neighbouring nuns drove in hordes
To hear settings of psalms
By Chopin and Brahms
And to come at the very first chords.

An influx of willowy Latins
Made a startling improvement to Matins
When they swayed down the aisle
Wearing either a smile
Or their clerical chiffons and satins.

"I'd like you to borrow this text
To work on before we have Sext.
Don't follow its strictures,
Just look at the pictures.
It should make a difference. Next!"

Two Cheers for Tramconductors

In Alexandria if you dare to catch a tram
It's not the only thing you catch. Omar Khayyam
Was right: "A jug, a loaf of bread, a pinch of ham,
A dose of this or that." (Or some such epigram).

A loaf of bread, a jug of wine? Many went jugless.
The bread was shared between the customs-men and smugglers.
But there was always "Thou", and soon there was Keith Douglas,
In spotless khaki with a figure like an hourglass.

His eyes were blue as cornflowers, cutting as a laser.
He bathed in asses' milk. His batman (G. S. Fraser)
Brought him his flagellator, shaving-cream and razor,
Ironed his shirt and licked the dandruff off his blazer.

"George, that's a filthy habit and I wish you'd kick it.
Pass me my cummerbund and pistol. I've a ticket
For one of Rommel's little hops. It won't be cricket,
Hitting those tanks for six on such a sandy wicket."

It did for him, of course. It did for Sidney Keyes.
But both together forced the Hun down on his knees.
Rommel advanced too far and left himself *en prise*.
They brought him into Alex where he lived on cheese.

Limburger made from crocodiles and Cairo gorgon-
zola seemed to satisfy his nasal organ.
His gaoler was a tramconductor: "Guten morgen!
I am very good friend of Forster, Edward Morgan.

"I serve you now my dear Herr Oberfeldwebel,
For since the war began my tram stays in her stable
And I am in the army. I shall lay the table
And bring as many kinds of cheese as I am able."

It's true, he worked the trams till he went off the rails,
For English reticence and all that it entails
Dampened his style: he'd dance the Dance of the Seven Veils
But Forster would look away and pare his fingernails.

He owned the unemended texts of all he penned:
Two Cheers for Tramconductors, *The Tramconductor's Friend*
And *Passage to Tramconductor* (we can recommend
The Longest Tramconductor and *Tramconductors End*).

"A loaf of bread, a whiff of cheese, a little bit
Of something else? You let me see your Messerschmitt?"
Such tactics Rommel was unwilling to commit
But unlike Forster couldn't get away from it.

"Take back your cheese! Take back your loaf of bread!
Remove your little bit of something else!" he said.
But all to no avail. They fell upon the bed:
There's nowhere that a tramconductor fears to tread.

Alexandria in wartime! Every café
Full of lieutenants with slim volumes of Cavafy,
Even the Arab Quarter was distinctly WAAFy
And Lawrence Durrell wore pyjamas in the NAAFI.

All the intense relationships became intenser,
And Desert Rats wore lipstick every night for ENSA.
Monty prepared hot chocolate for Bernard Spencer
(We are afraid this bit's been snipped out by the censor).

The tramconductors were the worst: their tooth-enamel
Gleamed broadly at the sight of any kind of mammal.
You'd find it hard to shake a tramconductor's trammel:
"A loaf of bread, a jug or two of wine, a camel . . ."

The war was over. It had been a great success.
Douglas and his kind were gone, but nonetheless
Their ghosts stayed on behind, in faultless battledress,
With tramconductors beside them in the wilderness.

Three Alpinists of Yesteryear

Three alpinists of yesteryear were climbing on one rope.
They'd started off at breakfast-time upon a gentle slope.
But now that it was afternoon the going had got rough.
They stopped to eat their sandwiches and thought they'd had enough.
They looked down on the valley at the Tyrolean scene
With onion spires and villages so neat and safe and clean.
They thought with some nostalgia of the life they'd left behind.
A *Mädchen* with a *Brötchen* was the life they had in mind.
Then one of them was puzzled by a funny distant sound.
It seemed someone was whispering to him deep from underground,
Saying:
You come along with crampons and you stick your pitons in.
You never ask permission though before you lads begin.
You bring me out in blotches. I've got gentians on me scalp.
You don't know the effect you're having on your little alp.

Our friend was rather worried that he might be going mad.
He wondered if his friends had heard the same as what he had.
He wanted so to mention it but thought that they might scoff.
Then the avalanche came rushing by and tossed his two friends off.
"My God," said he, "that's terrible. I'll have to clamber down.
I must inform their relatives when I get back to town.
How will I break the news to them how this disaster fell?
I rather wish the avalanche had tossed me off as well."
"Oh do you?" said the alp to him, "Well here's some more bad news,
You've lost your crampons, pitons, ropes and all the junk you use.
You're on your own from now, me lad. You'll not get back to sup
On a *Mädchen* with a *Brötchen* now. The only way is up.

You come along with crampons and you stick your pitons in.
You never ask permission though before you lads begin.
You bring me out in blotches. I've got gentians on me scalp.
You don't know the effect you're having on your little alp."

It was something like a chimney. It was something like a flue.
It was something like a funnel and a trifle slippery, too.
He climbed and climbed and tried to find a place where he could grip.
Then he disappeared within a kind of overhanging lip.
The villagers watched from below and gasped at what they saw.
His head, his shoulders, legs and boots went in and then—no more!
They found his dead companions beneath that fatal place
And noted how an ecstasy had frozen on each face.
They carried them to church that day and buried them in style
And when they came back out again the mountain seemed to smile.

They said:
"They come along with crampons and they stick their pitons in.
But they never ask permission though, these lads, when they begin.
They bring her out in blotches. She's got gentians on her scalp.
They don't know the effect they're having on our little alp."

Oh the alpinists of yesteryear were sturdy men and true
But they never quite accepted Alps can have their feelings too.
Their attitude to climbing was as selfish and as grim
As Edward Whymper's attitude to Mrs Whymper's whym.
And the moral of this story is both relevant and terse:
Next time you climb the Venusberg—ask permission first.
You know—
You come along with crampons and you stick your pitons in.
You never ask permission though before you lads begin.
You bring me out in blotches. I've got gentians on me scalp.
You don't know the effect you're having on your little alp.

The Red Light District Nurse

You'll see me park my car upon
A double yellow line.
The wardens doff their hats at me
And there's no clamp or fine,
For if you put the clamp on me
You drive off in a hearse.
   Don't mess around,
   Don't press around
The red light district nurse.

They trained me on the Reeperbahn.
They passed me in Amsterdam.
They crammed me in a uniform
(And there's quite a lot to cram).
They crammed and crammed until they found
I'd scored a double First.
   Anatomy?
   What's that to me?
I'm the red light district nurse.

The Local Health Authority
Supplies me with high heels
For going down on pensioners
Between the meals on wheels,
For my money's where my mouth is,
I don't put it in my purse.
   I get the feel of it
   And make a meal of it,
The red light district nurse.

What's wrong with you? I'll tell you, son.
You drank a bit too much
And went to the tattooist's shop
And redesigned your crotch.
You wonder what your wife will think.
If she's like me, she'll burst.
    Don't pester me.
    Say Yes to me!
The red light district nurse.

Two lesbots, one banana:
You have to tug and tug.
It's terrible when the fuse explodes
In an ancient one-pin plug,
But I'm there on time if they call me
And I put them in reverse.
    I've been through it myself.
    (I still do it myself!)
I'm the red light district nurse.

There were three drunken Irishmen
Who called on me one day.
They weren't on the National Health and so
I had to make them pay.
It was a straight two tricks with the first two Micks.
With the Fenian it was Erse.
    It's a hat-trick
    For St Patrick
And the red light district nurse.

I've customers who come to me
For a thorough rectal search
And I've patients who are satisfied
With sauna, tea and birch,
But some can take it out of you
And a few I call perverse
    (Colostomy?
    Get lost Tommy!)
I'm the red light district nurse!

Poem against Catholics

The boring executors approach their locks,
Fumbling with keys and more than halfway dense:
Sylvia Plath is given to C. B. Cox,
Lawrence to Leavis, Pope to Joseph Spence,
Pound to *Agenda*, Eliot to his wife,
Hopkins to Bridges and Kafka to Max Brod,
But Jesus gave the Church eternal life!
God we hate Catholics and their Catholic God.

It isn't that we'd rather someone who
Instead of singing simply says you it.
The whole palaver simply isn't true.
We'd not prefer a Quaker to a Jesuit.
But in the Proselytizing Handicap
The odds are heavy where they ride roughshod
And drive their spurs into the suffering map.
God we hate Catholics and their Catholic God.

Graham Greene finds them everywhere he travels
With submachineguns underneath their cassocks.
You can be certain, as the plot unravels,
They're smuggling opium in knee-worn hassocks.
Police-chiefs quote Pascal. Priests hit the bottle.
Strong men repent in Nishny-Novgorod.
The whole galère one could with pleasure throttle.
God we hate Catholics and their Catholic God.

The object of their worship makes us cross,
Since their employment of it is so gainful.
They sold off bits of it like candy-floss
(Surely the Romans meant it to be painful?).
Their tortured idols are so psychedelic
With gold and lapis artwork à la mode!
And nearly every thumbscrew is a relic.
God we hate Catholics and their Catholic goad.

They call their horrid children after saints
And educate them by such dubious means
They eagerly succumb to strange complaints
Or turn psychotic in their early teens.
"Ursula worries me," exclaims her mother.
"Her manner recently has been so odd.
I've *told* her she must *not* cremate her brother."
God we hate Catholics and their Catholic God.

See in the summerhouse where Father Flynn
Fingers his rosary and sets to work
Explaining why the Church holds it a sin:
"You mustn't ever hold it. That's called jerk-
ing off. Six *mea culpas*, Benedict."
He's coaching him for Ampleforth. Poor sod—
He'll get some education, we predict.
God we hate Catholics and their Catholic God.

"Not now," cries Mrs Macnamara, "*later!*"
When leapt on by her husband (what a beast).
"It says so on my Catholic calculator.
It also says so on my Catholic priest."
She'd do much better with a mortal coil
To spoil the child and spare the husband's rod.
Why don't they put a bill through in the Dàil?
God we hate Catholics and their Catholic God.

Their sheer resourcefulness one can't disparage.
External Combustion was their own invention,
So (indisputably) divorceless marriage
Which like a sardine key creates some tension
But *only once*. What moral supermen!
Or else what Paul said must have been a cod
Since those who marry twice must burn again.
God we hate Catholics and their Catholic God.

Rich English Catholics, busy doing good work
For filthy mission schools in fascist states.
Oily confessors crawling from the woodwork
With first-class tickets to the Pearly Gates.
How nice that Lady Priesthole looks so well.
She's left the housemaid's knee behind in Lourdes.
But where's the housemaid? God alone can tell.
God we hate Catholics and their Catholic Gourdes.

High Anglo-Catholics are beneath contempt—
All intellectual and moral wrecks.
They love the frills but hold themselves exempt
From all restrictions in the line of sex.
As press-ups are to health-fiends, genuflection
Is to the average Anglo-Catholic Prod.
What a good way to nourish one's erection!
God we hate Catholics and their Catholic God.

When Sister Flanagan from Houston, Texas,
Edited Baron Corvo for her Master's,
She changed the pronouns to reverse the sexes
As frills on chesterfields concealed their castors.
The text was passed unnoticed by the Syndics
And causes some confusion in the Bod.
Wait till she gets the Bible on the Index!
God we hate Catholics and their Catholic God.

A rugby-playing Catholic novelist,
Piers Paul Read, was lucky to be chosen
(Out of, we gather, a distinguished list)
To write about a new idea in frozen
Foods: a Rugby team crashed near Peru
On slopes the human toe had never trod
And ate each other. What a thing to do!
God—they ate Catholics and their Catholic God!

The Spectre

The King informed his court
  That he had planned
One afternoon a short
Excursion, to disport
  Upon the sand.

Accordingly some tents,
  A feather bed,
Some fowls and condiments
And eating implements
  Were sent ahead.

And in due time the King
  In gold enamel
With silver latticing
Set out from old Peiping
  Upon a camel.

The sea by half past four
  Was nearly boiling
And all along the shore
It creaked like an old door
  That needed oiling.

The princelings sat and gazed.
   It seemed they'd rather
Be at home. Amazed
At his resolve they praised
   The ancient father.

For there he danced. He thought a
   Dance was splendid
There beside the water.
And yet the dance was shorter
   Than he intended.

The sun began to spin
   Upon the sea
Which opened like a tin
To take it, sizzling, in
   Its custody.

His power of locomotion
   Began to seep
Away, the lulling ocean
Infused him like a potion.
   He fell asleep.

Out of his dreaming head
   They saw arise
A spectre of the dead
Who groaned aloud and said
   "It dies, all dies!"

The princelings knew which side
   Their bread was buttered.
They sat there at high-tide.
They sat there mortified
   And crossly muttered:

"Protocol in this sector
    Clearly worsens:
This unexpected spectre
Is sadly no respecter
    Of royal persons!"

They woke the King and whined:
    "It's time we went.
We don't suppose you'll mind.
When you want us you will find
    Us in the tent."

The King was neither enlightened
    Nor amused.
His adam's apple tightened.
In fact he was quite frightened
    And confused.

For there before him swayed
    The spectre which
Had sprung this ambuscade
Out of his head. It made
    His nostrils twitch.

"Everything dies, all dies!"
    The words were borne
Upon the wind, with flies
And sand and courtiers' cries
    All night, till dawn.

By then the court was jaded.
    With haggard eyes
The King looked just as they did,
Stared as the echoes faded:
    "All dies, all dies!"

And it was true, all true.
    King after king
Had wept to be a king all through
The long November nights and knew
    No solacing.

Vero got Vague, Vague got
    Astrap and Quile,
Astrap got Vague and Watt
While Quile got Fingersnot
    And Lavabile.

Lavabile got Vero,
    Vero got
Astrap and Vague and Vero,
Vague got Worpsle, Vero
    Got Fingersnot.

Fingersnot got Watt,
    Watt got Vague,
Vague got Quile and Watt
And Watt got Fingersnot
    And Quile got Vague.

And in the catacombs
    Each royal name
Inscribed in royal rooms
Deep in the royal tombs
    Was in the same name.

You might forget what you
    Were really called,
But one thing, at least, is true:
Old men, and babies too,
    Are often bald.

A dynasty had gone
    And this he knew,
And death took everyone.
But did it fall upon
    The future, too?

It did. And does. And thus
    We realise
However we make a fuss
It does not stop with us:
    "All dies, all dies."

The past is not enough
    To satisfy
Its greed. However tough,
Just try to call its bluff:
    You die. All die.

And so the King, with slaves
    In close attendance,
Set out across the waves
To weep upon the graves
    Of his descendants.

Two Hysterical Phantasies on the Names of Poets

'The cosy phallocentric world of contemporary
British poetry will be shattered next spring by two
collections of poetry by Wendy Cope and Fiona Pitt-Kethley,
distinct voices united by their frank and funny view
of sexual relations.'
                    Observer Magazine, 29 DECEMBER 1985

I

When the plums are in bloom in Dolgellau,
And the Mawddach is teeming with fish,
I shall marry Fiona Pitt-Kethley
And accede to her every wish.

I'll be good. I'll be graceful and moral.
I'll wear suits and I'll sometimes wear socks.
When Fiona says: "You! Prune that laurel!"
I shall not take it out on the phlox.

We shall live with her folks down at Buddleigh,
Where the butterflies nuzzle the buddleia.
When Fiona trills: "Time to get cuddly!"
I'll get more than that. I shall get cuddlier.

And her father, the Major, God bless him,
Every time he comes home from the pub,
I shall help poor Fiona undress him.
She can give me his blankets to scrub.

Her mother's so hail-fellow-well-met,
Her handshake is pure Black and Decker.
She wears khaki shorts and pith helmet
And tells you to keep up your pecker.

Her brothers I think I can handle.
There's Pogo and Mimsey and Gob.
Pogo's Togo job ended in scandal.
Gob's not quite the full—you know—two bob.

Old Mimsey's a bit of a loner,
Though he's in very thick with the vicar.
In fact, as I hear from Fiona,
He could hardly be in that much thicker.

I'm not quite so sure of the sisters.
They've all taken vows—quite right too.
To cloisters, from Klosters and clysters—
I think that sounds healthy, don't you?

Now the plums are in bloom in Dollgellau
And I must have gone quite off my head.
JESUS CHRIST! Here's Fiona Pitt-Kethley!
I'll go jump in the Mawddach instead.

2

Can Wendy cope?
I hope she can.
She's got the soap
To please her man.

Wendy's no dope,
No also-ran.
Give her the rope,
She'll noose her man.

Her trap's a trope,
Her man's a fan,
She won't say Nope,
Nor will her man.

The love of Pope
For Lutheran,
Of philanthrope
For hooligan,

Of antelope
For marzipan,
Has lesser scope,
I grant you, than

The lion's lope,
The spider's span
Or heliotrope
Of old Japan.

But when you grope
Her cardigan
The vistas ope
On summer's tan:

O envelope!
O tongues that scan
The slippery slope
Of creel and cran!

Wendy can cope,
I know she can.
Up, periscope!
And down, divan!

The Dream within the Dream

I dreamed the vultures came for me
And they knew what to do.
'Cause when I woke I knew that I'd
   Lost most of what
   There was of me:
It was like a dream come true.

What other people dream about
Is nice, or so it seems.
Am I the only one who has
These dreams within these dreams?

Oh tip me quickly out of bed
And tickle me till I scream,
But wake me from the dream within
   The dream within
   The dream within
The dream within the dream.

I dreamed that my oesophagus
Was lived in by a stoat,
And when I woke I found that I
   Had something like
   A weasel or
A hedgehog in my throat.
     Oh Lord,
A hedgehog in my throat.

Oh scrub my soul with brillo pads
And hose me down with cream,
But wake me from the dream within
   The dream within
   The dream within
The dream within the dream.

I dreamed my teeth were made of glass
And shattered in the night
And when I woke, the looking glass
   Looked back at me
   And said to me
There's not a fang in sight.
      Oh Lord,
There's not a fang in sight.

So chop me up like chocolate chips
And smash my self-esteem,
But wake me from the dream within
   The dream within
   The dream within
The dream within the dream.

Give me a dish of dynamite,
A tot of TNT,
Give me a slosh of cyanide,
   A glug of drug,
   A mug of slug
Or some new therapy.
      Oh Lord,
Or some new therapy.

Yes, tie me to the railroad track
Or something more extreme,
But wake me from the dream within
   The dream within
   The dream within
The dream within the dream.
         Oh Lord,
The dream within the dream.

Born Too Soon

All the opportunities we miss by being born too soon!
All the pleasures of the evening lost by going to bed at noon!
Lydgate never peeled an orange, Langland never bit a Mars.
Chaucer might have felt quite raffish if he'd learned to smoke cigars.
   Born too soon, born too soon.

Bullough's *Sources* might have meant that Shakespeare's plots were
                                                more than cursory.
Marlowe never had the chance to bank a large Arts Council Bursary.
Herrick's sweet disorder counts for nothing in an age of zips.
Penicillin might have strengthened Davenant's relationships.
   Born too soon, born too soon.

Donne avoided death duties and Rochester a parking ticket.
Marvell would have simply *loved* a day or two of country cricket.
Richard Crashaw yearned in vain for something like a heart transplant.
Joseph Addison just missed becoming the first agony aunt.
   Born too soon, born too soon.

Poor old Milton, locked in darkness: not by bribery or stealth
Could he procure, like A. N. Wilson, glasses on the National Health,
Nor Pope, when furnishing his grotto, quantities of garden gnomes.
Swift's work suffers from his ignorance of missing chromosomes.
   Born too soon, born too soon.

Fanny Burney needed pretty coloured jackets from Virago.
Blake and Smart would have been quite at home in *Poetry* (Chicago).
Gray, if sex had been invented, would have found the knowledge bliss.
William Cowper needed several years of deep analysis.
   Born too soon, born too soon.

Dorothy at Grasmere might have triumphed with a Hoovermatic,
William saved his quill enlarging snaps of Keswick in the attic.
Samuel needed fees for talking? Why not join the BBC?
Sara might have welcomed Sam, getting kicks from being three
   Born too soon, born too soon.

Shelley would have benefited from aerobics and from jogging,
Listerine have justified the urgency of Keats's snogging.
Byron never used a Pentax, posing Arab boys in Cairo
(More of Donny Johnny might have surfaced if he'd used a biro).
   Born too soon, born too soon.

Branwell Brontë never had to face his sisters' querying gaze
When another undergardener left the vicarage in a haze.
(Housebound Cathy found that Heathcliff somewhat cramped her
                             social range:
"Wuthering Heights Two-Seven: Operator, give me
                         Thrushcross Grange!")
   Born too soon, born too soon.

Arnold missed the tape recorder, Tennyson the silver screen,
Robert Browning never saw a peepshow of the kind we mean.
Television would have ushered Dickens into *every* home.
Edward Lear's existence might have been transformed by
                             shaving foam.

   Born too soon, born too soon.

T. S. Eliot had (and missed) the chance to go and toss the caber
But he never saw his musical provide a float for Faber.
Hopkins could have read his stuff (with scansion marks) on Radio 3.
Rudyard Kipling could have eaten Mr Kipling cakes for tea.
   Born too soon, born too soon.

Think of what we're losing now by having come to birth too soon:
All the future we imagine, haunting as a honeymoon.
You and us, like them, would gladly have performed it with impunity,
That delightful, stimulating, tragic, missing opportunity.
   Born too soon, born too soon.

The Terrible Devotional Mystery
of Martin Dodsworth

"On a huge Hill,
Cragged, and steep, Truth stands..."
(JOHN DONNE)

"Fault!" (JOAN HUNTER DUNNE)

For whom this erithistic throbbing of
The buds? The penitential disembowelling?
For whom this craven blood flowing in love,
As thin as Cranmer's, vigorous as towelling?
Who crouches at the net, his mouth compressed
Severely to a little Gothic slit?
Who but my disciplined disciple, blest
In being harmless and not knowing it?

Let the man worship. Let him stand and serve
The grizzled Offa that he can't refuse.
Hermits wolf down the scraps that they deserve,
And wear like robes the tortures that they choose.
Frowning in joy, my nailed hand makes its motion:
Now who returns my balls with such devotion?

The Land of Leery Looks

In the land of leery looks
All the pubs have inglenooks.
Swans are geese. The rest are rooks
In the land of leery looks.

See the harvest stacked in stooks!
Smell the onions hung from hooks!
Taste the turtles brought from brooks
In the land of leery looks!

In the land of leery looks
All the geniuses are crooks
And all the poets cook the books
In the land of leery looks.

Die Minze-Ernte

Das Minzemädl kündigt an.
Die Minze-Ernte ist getan.
Die Kinder spielen in der Ernte.
Die gelbe Kuh frisst die Placenta.

The Sexy Old Ladies
Of Havergo Hill

The sexy old ladies of Havergo Hill,
They never let go of the stick.
It's an absolute proof of the triumph of will.
They get what they want and they're wanting it still.
That's why Margo Margoulies is still on the pill:
At a hundred, she knows every trick.

I said to my son as I straightened his tie:
"When you're dining with Granny, take care.
If she brings out the Bols, mind you say with a sigh
'I've some homework to finish. I really must fly.'"
But he came back next day with a gleam in his eye
And some pieces of straw in his hair.

The Havergo milkmen look tired and drawn.
They've taken to going in pairs.
The plumber is wild-eyed. His trousers are torn.
"I can service a Hotpoint," he says with a yawn.
"But it seems a bit much to be called out at dawn
And the Hotpoint's up two flights of stairs."

For many, a giggling games-room tussle
Was their very first taste of sin,
With Stopes in the dorm: "The vagina's a *muscle*."
Quite a few spent a week-end with Bertrand Russell
And some are so old they came out with the bustle
And never quite got back in.

It wasn't a question of wedding bells
And a white first night in Paris.
There are endless lists of men and hotels
In their memoirs (and almost nothing else):
It was ten in the morning with H. G. Wells
And just after lunch with Frank Harris.

The next generation were hardly the same,
Lytton and Morgan and Ivor.
Nor did Wystan and Christopher quite play the game.
The old ladies were old, there was no one to blame,
And they finally just had to conquer their shame
And hand Dylan Thomas a fiver.

Now it's all systems go on Havergo Hill.
The parties buzz on round the clock.
If it breathes, and wears trousers, they move in for the kill.
They've invited Karl Miller, but he's feeling ill.
No wonder: his hostess knew John Stuart Mill
And she's broken the bathroom lock.

The Ape at the End of the Phone

I tried to send my love to you
By Electronic Mail.
They returned my Prestel Smoochogram:
Why do I always fail?
I want to blow a kiss to you
But I find my cover's blown.
I'm worse than hit-or-miss to you.
I'm the Ape at the End of the Phone.

They handed me an Apple.
It yielded twenty bytes
And yet I went bananas
When I had you in my sights.
An Apricot was thrust at me
But it only made me groan.
I never thought you trusted me.
I'm the Ape at the End of the Phone.

I lifted the receiver:
There was nothing to receive.
I'm the original Old Adam
And you're the original Eve.
I'm Joseph and you're Mary
And yet I feel alone.
Is it because I'm hairy?
I'm the Ape at the End of the Phone.

I thought that my insistence
Would charm the operator,
But when I order: "Long Distance!"
She tells me to ring back later.
I've tried the gentlest murmur.
I've used a megaphone.
It's a Birmingham number, not Burma.
I'm going Ape at the End of this Phone.

PARTINGTIME HALL

Partingtime Hall

A Film Script

I

He stepped off the platform and into eternity,
Only sixteen and a future so bright,
The heir to a fortune so large he could burn it, he
Could have bought Ferdinand Marcos outright.

The press was ablaze with the curse of the Schruijkers:
DAD DROWNS IN LAKE, NOW SON FALLS UNDER TRAIN!
They shot at the mother with motorised Leicas,
They blew up her face and they blew up her pain.

She came for the funeral, veiled and in sables.
The scent was so strong that it made your heart race.
A whiff of musk-rose with a hint of the stables,
A dash of what beavers bite off in the chase.

The Head took her arm up the aisle and he murmured:
"We thought you'd like lunch at the Partingtime Arms.
I've given you over to Mr McDiarmid.
He coached Paul last year when he flunked on the Psalms."

"The da-ay Thou ga-avest Lo-ord is ended . . ."
The standard of singing was all you could wish.
The Chaplain's encomium really was splendid.
He almost implied that young Paul was a dish.

The Captain of Hockey, the Captain of Rugger
And four perfect prefects bore Paul to his grave.
"Sod this job," said the Head Pre. "This coffin's a bugger.
Do you think she might tip us? I feel like a rave."

They threw in his colours. She tossed in some roses.
Then Mr McDiarmid appeared at her side.
He gave her a squeeze as they both dabbed their noses,
Then steered her away through the press like a bride.

They made their escape in McDiarmid's two-seater,
Which he took down the lanes just as fast as he dared.
The short-cut was neat, the haircut was neater.
His trousers and nostrils were equally flared.

The Partingtime Arms is a sea of chintz sofas,
Oak cradles with pot-plants and grandfather clocks.
There's an annexe with Ploughman's for ploughmen and chauffeurs
While Mum's brought the menu with rum-on-the-rocks.

The chef learned his trade from a plausible maître
Who taught him the rules of the latest cuisine,
Fundamentally stingy, more néant than être:
A raspberry gravy with half a French bean.

McDiarmid had tact. As he toyed with his coulis,
He watched her recover in fits and in starts:
He knew her emotions had been put through a mouli.
Her cheeks were like goat's cheese or chicory tarts.

He started to comfort her after the widgeon
(Half a breast each, in a sauna of pears)
With a dash of philosophy, crumbs of religion
And a freckled left hand with a fuzz of red hairs.

The endive was curly, with sesame dressing,
The redcurrant sorbet was willing and damp,
The water boiled up as their knees started pressing
And fell back as coffee when he blew out the lamp.

II

"Oh Mr McDiarmid? So kind at the funeral..."
(Her lips at the mouth-piece) "... what would I have done...
And yet I believe it was fated that sooner or l-
ater we'd meet... all you did for my son.

"So much we must talk about" (crooned the receiver)
"I feel that there's something unique that we share.
I've sent you your ticket. We'll meet at Geneva.
You know Paul was all for inviting you there."

The head saw the point of the kind invitation:
McDiarmid had not been himself since the death,
"Besides, there is only a week to vacation.
I can manage to hem all the kilts for *Macbeth*."

III

He felt fairly svelte as he proferred his passport
And strolled through the gate to the Baggage Reclaim
But the clasps of his case hadn't done what a clasp ought
And the burst-open contents revolved to his shame:

It wasn't the nightgown or volume of Virgil
But the special effects he had smuggled along:
A knowing young nun gave him back his Defergel
(Though he had to disown the cerise wet-look thong).

Lolly Schruijker looked striking in white at the barrier.
Her chauffeur looked insolent, tailored in blue,
As if to say, Do you expect me to carry a
Suitcase like *that* for a chancer like *you*?

The car was a Vulva and snug as a thimble,
The trim could have cost almost any amount:
Kid arm-rests, smoked glass and cologne on a gimbal,
As private and lush as a numbered account.

As they drove to the Château, his hostess was chattering,
Her nails on his blazer. Alert as a lynx!
He was shown to his room. Its dimensions were shattering.
He showered and gargled, then swanned down to drinks.

"I'd hoped we'd eat out." "Really? that would be splendid!"
"But Anton is certain a storm will soon break.
You can't see the French side: the mist has descended.
So tiresome. You just can't rely on this lake."

At the end of the meal Anton laid out the Pflumli.
"What's this?" "Brandy." "Hmm." "But it's made out of plums.
You don't *have* to . . ." "I'd love to . . ." The butler went off gloomily.
McDiarmid's eyes watered. "Hot stuff!'" he said. "Crumbs!"

Stuffed elks, shields and antlers, dim trophies with handles,
Lost legends and mottoes, the husband's bequest,
Reflections in glass, stalactites from the candles,
One eyeball, two eyeballs, a hostess, a guest.

"Oh, Mr McDiarmid. . . . Well, Mr McDiarmid!
No, Mr McDiarmid! *Ow!!* Mr McDiarm—"
He looks faintly troubled. His trousers confirm it,
Projecting a map of Australia in sperm.

IV

Next morning, he gingerly stepped on the jetty.
The mountains hung over his hungover brain
And their peaks in reflection made passion seem petty
And the previous night's pounce absolutely insane.

He loosened the painter and pushed out the dinghy.
The breakfasting waves took a slurp at the prow.
He had a slight problem: *one* oar in each thingy—
And he knew he'd to pull, and go backward, but *how*?

She was feeding the swans from the end of the terrace
With a bagful of yesterday's croissants and rolls,
While Anton laid breakfast: hot chocolate and cherries,
Bresaola and Gruyère and profiteroles.

He noticed the swans moving in, a flotilla.
Their radar homed in on each depth-charge of bread.
Every bird was a threat, every beak was a killer.
She perfected her range and a crust hit his head.

"Good morning!" "Oh, there you are..." "Wasn't it frightful?"
"Wasn't what?" "Oh, the *storm*!" "I suppose so..." "Don't say
You didn't hear?" "Oh, I was out like a light, full
Of... what was it called?" "Pflumli." "God!..." "That's OK.

"I was actually flattered. Such things don't occur, you
Must realise, out here. Yes, you know what I mean!
Stop brooding! It's OK! You weren't *going*, were you?
I've given your trousers to Anton to clean."

V

You minx, thought McDiarmid, as he tied up the painter,
Though her mood had now changed like the mood of the lake.
She was quiet and thoughtful. Her smile had grown fainter.
It seemed she had some proposition to make.

"There's a thing—oh, it's ghastly—I can't bear the thought of it.
I just don't know where to begin with Paul's room.
I haven't been in there. I know that I ought've. It
Seems such a business. It fills me with gloom."

McDiarmid's eyes narrowed. "You mean, Paul's possessions?
They're just as he left them? Poor Lolly. I see.
It's hard on your own to throw off these obsessions.
No, no, I insist! You must leave it to me!"

She gave him a glance that was girlish and grateful.
She offered to help him, but he said: "No way."
He'd done this before. It was hard. It was hateful.
But it had to be done at the end of the day.

He crumpled his napkin and rose from the table.
He was firm as a journalist hot on a scoop.
He asked his directions from Anton, unable
To credit his luck in this chance of a snoop.

VI

Where would Paul have kept them? He hoped they were hidden.
They had to be found, or they'd say what they knew.
The room was a graveyard, a sort of a midden,
As clear as a dig in an aerial view:

The geometry set with the missing dividers,
The flexible rule from his O-Level phase,
Approvals and hinges and balsa-wood gliders,
The sticky remains of a brief Airfix craze.

The harlequin slumped in its tangle of cotton,
Much-frayed fluffy friends, irredeemably dead,
The books he'd grown out of on shelves and forgotten,
The books he'd grown into right there by the bed:

Selected John Ashbery, Schuyler, O'Hara,
Gravity's Rainbow, and *End as A Man*,
Young Torless, Cavafy and others bizarrer,
Lord Weary, Das Schloss, Lady Windermere's Fan—

"And all with my bookplate!" (Mountgracechurch McDiarmid—
The boys called him "Mounty"; the staff called him "Grace"—
Three pelicans passant, a thing like a mermaid,
A motto whose Latin fell flat on its face).

"Did I lend him all these? Did he read them?" he muttered,
"It's rather a challenging list to get through."
He picked up the Wilde. From its pages there fluttered
Two opera-stubs for *The Turn of the Screw*.

He remembered the evening, the Miller production,
The rush up to London, the crush at the bar,
The face at the window, the ghosts of seduction,
The cold cherry soup in the old Gay Hussar.

It was then that it happened, without his volition.
It was then that he knew things had got out of hand,
From a brief awkward pause to a deep intuition,
A dangerous game, unforeseen and unplanned.

The boy was returning to be with his mother
(His father had drowned early on in the term)
And one kind of comforting leads to another
As any experienced arm will confirm.

Paul left the next morning, and thanked him so sweetly.
His letters began to arrive every day.
McDiarmid replied, and replied indiscreetly.
He was proud of his prose and got carried away.

It was fun for a while, but a week or two after,
As the trunks were unloaded at Partingtime Halt
And the smoking compartments exploded with laughter
And the nude in the toilet was nobody's fault

And the plunge baths were filled with a rumble of plumbing
And the steam in the changing-room wept down the wall
To the wail of Toshibas and barely-tuned strumming,
There were tears in the study at Partingtime Hall.

McDiarmid had cooled. All he saw was the danger.
He had to draw back or he might lose his post.
Paul had needed a friend. What he met was a stranger,
Merely Mounty again, when he'd needed him most.

There is loss in a look, there is sorrow in seeking,
There's a drop on the page and its savour is salt.
There's a phone in the staff-room, the constable speaking:
"There's a boy on the tracks down at Partingtime Halt!"

VII

He shuddered a little and tore up the tickets.
"*The Turn of the Screw*," he remarked. "That was apt.
Now where are those letters? I'd better be quick, it's
The one opportunity, or I'll be strapped."

He started to look in the obvious places.
The desk drawers were jammed with old essays and books.
A knock at the door. It was Anton, with cases:
"Madame sent you these." He gave one of his looks.

Left alone once again, he scoured section by section
As seekers of treasure lay grids on a field.
From corners to centre he scoured to perfection,
But those risqué epistles remained unrevealed.

And the cases filled up and the room was denuded
And pimples of bluetack were left on the wall.
If the letters weren't there, then (McDiarmid concluded),
The boy must have thrown them away after all.

He walked up and down: could the parquet be lifted?
He felt in the marquetry desk for a drawer.
He pushed the tiled stove, but it couldn't be shifted.
Then he knew he was watched: she was there, at the door.

"It's as if you had killed him." "What? Lolly, how could you?"
"I mean, all that life—you've just packed it away."
"You did *ask* me." "I'm sorry. Be kind to me, would you?
"I can't tell you how much I've been dreading this day."

She came to his arms like a child to a towel,
All shivering and blue and in need of a hug.
He laid on the charm, laid it on with a trowel,
And her eyelids grew heavy as if from a drug.

She wouldn't let him go, he wouldn't let her go.
They fell on the bearskin and their skins entwined.
He took her obliquely, her took her a tergo,
He took her in every niche he could find.

And in every room, every time they were able,
From terrace to turret, from attic to vault,
From bearskin to bed to the billiard table,
They mocked at the phantom of Partingtime Halt.

The spell had been long. It was time now to break it.
McDiarmid had practised the sculls every day.
He invited her out for a trip on the lake. It
Was time now to say all the things he must say.

"It was wonderful, Lolly. I mean it. No, really.
I'll treasure the memory as long as I live.
You exist so intensely. You pay for it dearly,
And still at the end you have so much to give."

"'At the end'?" She looked blank. "Mounty, don't be so silly.
You're not going back to that awful old place."
"I *have* to." "Why? Brrr . . . Now I'm feeling quite chilly.
Let's go home," she exclaimed, with a dainty grimace.

It was time to be tough. "Lolly, listen, my dearest—"
"DON'T PATRONISE ME!" It was just as he thought:
She would go off the deep end at even the merest
Suggestion he wouldn't behave as he ought.

VIII

"Lolly—" "STOP IT!" "My job, Lolly!" How she was shrieking
And weeping and stopping her ears with her palms.
The water was choppy, the rowlocks were creaking.
McDiarmid leaned forward, took hold of her arms,

And said: "Listen." She shook herself free: "No, *you* listen,
You vulgar young man, don't you push me too far."
The rage through her tears made her irises glisten.
"I know what your type is. I know what you are."

"And what might that be?" Now McDiarmid was nettled.
Her laughter was sudden. It came and it went.
"You must have forgotten. You've got some unsettled
Affairs, you remember? Those letters you sent?

I've got them, of course. Did you think I might lose them?
My lawyer's instructed. The moment you're gone,
A phone call from me and he'll know how to use them.
I'm afraid you're the prisoner. This is Chillon."

McDiarmid laughed. "Lolly, you are so preposterous.
When *I* tell the world what *you* did with young Paul,
Do you think they'll admire you? My dear, you'll be ostrac-
ized. Think of the scandal!... What's that, then—one-all?"

He gloated. She coloured. "I never!" "Now, Lolly,
It's all there in writing. The child was upset.
He told all the details. So touching!—but folly.
If you do things like that you deserve what you get."

She screamed as she stood up: "No! What are you saying?"
He reached out to grapple her down—a mistake.
They fought for a moment, unbalanced and swaying,
Then the dinghy capsized and they fell in the lake.

She wouldn't let him go, he couldn't let her go.
She clung for dear life but she clung like a shroud
And they sank through the world where the mourners and myrrh go,
Through the waves, through the wharfs, through the weltering crowd

Of the drowned, of the drifting, the drugged and the driven,
White fingers extended and bubbles for breath,
Unmourned, unrepentant, unloved, unforgiven,
A total immersion course ending in death.

The siren went up. The hydraulic doors lifted.
The lifeboat was triggered and shot from the chute.
It skimmed down the lake where the dinghy had drifted
And circled the scene of their fatal dispute.

From a terrace a mile off a telescope glinted.
On the eye at the eyepiece, as cold as blue steel,
The film of the lake was developed and printed.
Anton picked up the house-phone and cancelled the meal.

IX

The last summer tourists are quitting the canton.
The Sotheby's agent is making a list,
Sticking numbers on Braques. There's a number on Anton.
There's a gap in the inventory. Something's been missed.

And at Partingtime Hall there's a queue for the bursary
Where incomes from covenants turn into sweets.
The boys don't suspect, being fresh from the nursery,
How allowances bolster the school's balance-sheets.

The chauffeurs are waiting, the mothers are weeping,
The gravel is deep on the drive to the gate.
No tears before bed-time, no tousle-haired sleeping
Or shout up the banisters: "Johnny, it's late!"

Instead, over villa and mews-flat and rectory,
A mysterious warning is heard to appall:
"You cannot escape from Fate's tragic trajectory,
Put down in the cradle for Partingtime Hall."

For grief's a seducer with fur on his collar
And love is a child who steps into a car.
At Partingtime Hall it's a dime to a dollar
A love and a grief will find out who they are.

For love comes to grief like a gull to an oilslick,
And where is the solvent to salvage its wings?
Where the kiss for the frog? Where the dogs who Job's boils lick?
And where are the tweezers to pluck out the stings?

He stepped off the platform and out of the triangle.
Look what a trail he has left in his wake—
Grief to compare with the grief of the Dying Gaul,
One corpse on the rails and two more by the lake.

So come all you parents and pity these spectres,
Give heed to the heart-stopping story of Paul.
Don't buy that yearbook. Tear up the prospectus.
Don't send your children to Partingtime Hall.